I Can Practice Writing
Cursive

Brighter Child ®
An imprint of Carson-Dellosa Publishing LLC
P.O. Box 35665
Greensboro, NC 27425 USA

Printed in Minster, OH USA • All rights reserved.   ISBN 0-7696-2858-3

9 10 11 12 13 GLO 15 14 13 12 11 10   189107784

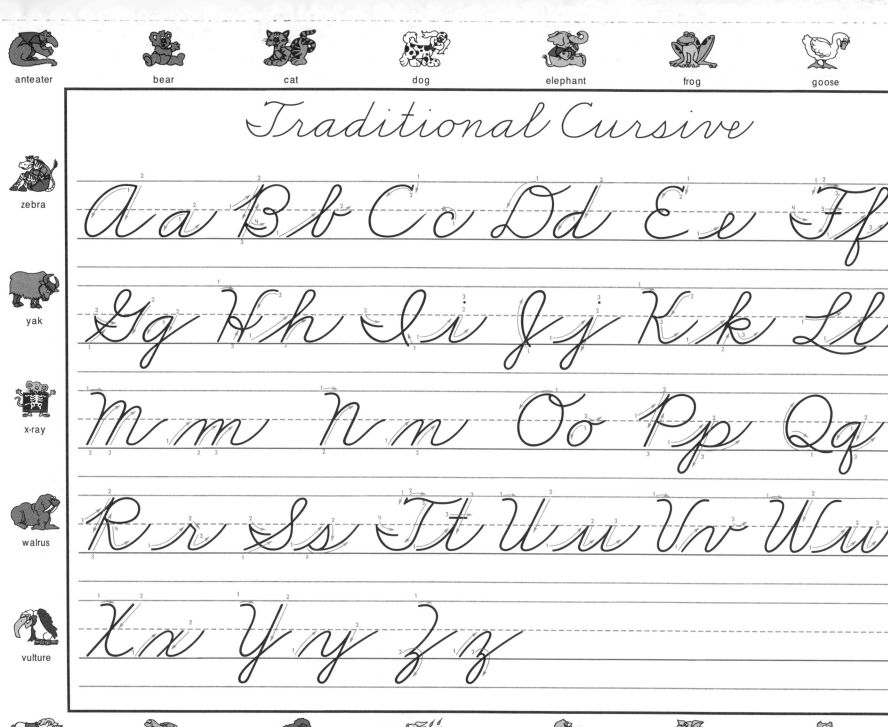

Traditional Cursive

anteater
bear
cat
dog
elephant
frog
goose
hippopotamus
zebra
iguana
yak
jaguar
x-ray
kangaroo
walrus
lion
vulture
monkey

unicorn
turtle
squirrel
rabbit
quail
pig
owl
numbat

Let's Warm Up!

Practice by tracing the lines.

Name _____

Practice by tracing the lines.

Name _____

Let's Warm Up!

Practice by tracing the lines.

Name _____

Practice by tracing the lines.

Name _____

Practice by tracing the lines.

Name _____

Let's Warm Up!

Practice by tracing the lines.

Name _____

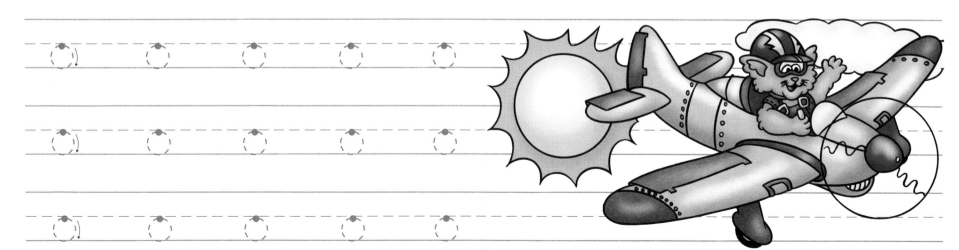

Practice by tracing the words and numbers.
Then write the words and numbers.

Name _____

one 1

two 2

three 3

four 4

five 5

Practice by tracing the words and numbers.
Then write the words and numbers.

Name _____

six 6

seven 7

eight 8

nine 9

ten 10

Numbers

Practice by tracing the words and numbers.
Then write the words and numbers.

Name _____

eleven 11

twelve 12

thirteen 13

fourteen 14

fifteen 15

Practice by tracing the words and numbers.
Then write the words and numbers.

Name _____

sixteen 16

seventeen 17

eighteen 18

nineteen 19

twenty 20

Shape Words

Practice by tracing the words.
Then write the words.

Name _____

square

circle

rectangle

oval

Color Words

Practice by tracing the words.
Then write the words.

Name _____

red

blue

yellow

orange

Practice by tracing the words.
Then write the words.

Name _____

black

white

purple

pink

Practice by tracing the words.
Then write the words.

Name _____

brown

gray

green

Complete this sentence:

My favorite color

is _____.

Practice Page

Practice writing on your own.

Name _____

Practice Page

Practice writing on your own.

Name _____

Practice writing on your own.

Name _____

Practice writing on your own.

Name _____

Practice writing on your own.

Name _____

Practice writing on your own.

Name _____

Practice writing on your own.

Name _____

Practice Page

Practice writing on your own.  Name _____

Practice by tracing the words and abbreviations. Then write the words and abbreviations.

Name _____

Sunday

Sun.

Monday

Mon.

Practice by tracing the words and abbreviations. Then write the words and abbreviations.

Name _____

Tuesday

Tues.

Wednesday

Wed.

Practice by tracing the words and abbreviations. Then write the words and abbreviations.

Name _____

Thursday

Thurs.

Friday

Fri.

Practice by tracing the words and abbreviations. Then write the words and abbreviations.

Name _____

Saturday

Sat.

Today

Practice by tracing the words and abbreviations. Then write the words and abbreviations.

Name _____

January

Jan.

February

Feb.

Practice by tracing the words and abbreviations. Then write the words and abbreviations.

Name _____

March

Mar.

April

Apr.

Practice by tracing the words and abbreviations. Then write the words and abbreviations.

Name _____

May

June

July

August

Aug.

Practice by tracing the words and abbreviations. Then write the words and abbreviations.

Name _____

September

Sept.

October

Oct.

Months of the Year and Abbreviations

Practice by tracing the words and abbreviations. Then write the words and abbreviations.

Name _____

November

Nov.

December

Dec.

Practice writing on your own.

Name _____

Practice writing on your own.

Name _____

Practice writing on your own.

Name _____

Practice writing on your own.

Name _____

Practice Page

Practice writing on your own.

Name _____

Practice writing on your own.

Name _____

Practice writing on your own.

Name _____

Practice writing on your own.

Name _____

Practice by tracing the words.
Then write the words.

Name _____

winter

spring

summer

fall

Weather Words

Practice by tracing the words.
Then write the words.

Name _____

snow

rain

sunshine

sleet

Complete this sentence:

Today we have

Holidays

Practice by tracing the words.
Then write the words.

Name _____

Halloween

Easter

Fourth of July

Hanukkah

Practice by tracing the words.
Then write the words.

Name _____

Christmas

Thanksgiving

Kwanza

Happy Birthday

School Words

Practice by tracing the words.
Then write the words.

Name _____

gym

playground

classroom

principal's office

Practice by tracing the words.
Then write the words.

Name _____

math

music

art

gym

Practice by tracing the words.
Then write the words.

Name _____

science

spelling

social studies

writing

Practice by tracing the words.
Then write the words.

Name _____

teacher

aide

nurse

principal

Practice writing on your own.

Name _____

Practice writing on your own.

Name _____

Practice writing on your own.

Name _____

Practice writing on your own.

Name _____

Practice writing on your own.

Name _____

Practice Page

Practice writing on your own.

Name _____

Practice writing on your own.

Name _____

Practice writing on your own.

Name _____

Practice by tracing the words.
Then write the words.

Name _____

pencil

book

folder

paper

Safety Words

Practice by tracing the words.
Then write the words.

Name _____

stop

go

caution

Family Words

Practice by tracing the words.
Then write the words.

Name _____

Mother

Father

Mom

Practice by tracing the words.
Then write the words.

Name _____

Dad

Grandma

Grandpa

Practice by tracing the words.
Then write the words.

Name _____

aunt

uncle

brother

sister

Write the names of the people in your family.

Name _____

Neighborhood Words

Practice by tracing the words.
Then write the words.

Name _____

street

road

store

theater

Practice by tracing the words.
Then write the words.

Name _____

apartment

library

office

park

Complete these sentences:

Name _____

I live in a

_____.

My address is

_____.

Write a sentence about your neighborhood:

Practice by tracing the words.
Then write the words.

Name _____

dollar $

cents ¢

penny 1¢

Practice by tracing the words.
Then write the words.

Name _____

nickel 5¢

dime 10¢

quarter 25¢

Money Words

Practice by tracing the words.
Then write the words.

Name _____

_____

- - - - - - - - - - - - - - - - - - -

_____

_____

- - - - - - - - - - - - - - - - - - -

_____

_____

- - - - - - - - - - - - - - - - - - -

_____

_____

- - - - - - - - - - - - - - - - - - -

_____

_____

- - - - - - - - - - - - - - - - - - -

_____

_____

- - - - - - - - - - - - - - - - - - -

_____

_____

- - - - - - - - - - - - - - - - - - -

_____

_____

- - - - - - - - - - - - - - - - - - -

_____

_____

- - - - - - - - - - - - - - - - - - -

_____

Practice writing on your own.

Name _____

Practice writing on your own.

Name _____

Practice writing on your own.

Name _____

Practice writing on your own.

Name _____

Practice Page

Practice writing on your own.

Name _____

Practice Page

Practice writing on your own.

Name _____

Practice writing on your own.

Name _____

Practice Page

Practice writing on your own.

Name _____

Action Words

Practice by tracing the words.
Then write the words.

Name _____

run

swim

jump

fly

Practice by tracing the words.
Then write the words.

Name _____

sing

read

play

study

Adjectives

Practice by tracing the words.
Then write the words.

Name _____

big

long

tall

good

Write the correct adjective next to the picture.

Name _____

tall

taller

tallest

Write the correct adjective next to the picture.

Name _____

big

bigger

biggest

_____

_____

Comparison Adjectives

Write the correct adjective next to the picture.

Name _____

small

smaller

smallest

Comparison Adjectives

Write the correct adjective next to the picture.

Name _____

long

longer

longest

Write the correct adjective next to the picture.

Name _____

good

better

best

Comparison Adjectives

Write the correct comparative adjective in the blank.

Name _____

I had the _____ time
(good)

ever. David is _____
(tall)

than Susan. It was

the _____ kitten
(small)

I had ever seen. I ate

the _____ ice cream
(big)

sundae.

87

Practice by tracing the words.
Then write the words.

Name _____

Dear

Thank you

Sincerely

Your friend

Practice writing on your own.

Name _____

Practice writing on your own.

Name _____

Practice Page

Practice writing on your own.

Name _____

Practice writing on your own.

Name _____

Practice writing on your own.

Name _____

Practice writing on your own.

Name _____

Practice Page

Practice writing on your own.

Name _____

Practice writing on your own.

Name _____

Practice by tracing the words.
Then write the words.

Name _____

dictionary

definition

alphabetical order

Pronouns

Practice by tracing the words.
Then write the words.

Name _____

I

me

you

her

we

Practice by tracing the words.
Then write the words.

Name _____

he

she

they

them

Contractions

Practice by tracing the words.
Then write the words.

Name _____

I'll

she'll

we'll

you'll

Language Arts Words

Practice by tracing the words.
Then write the words.

Name _____

sentence

paragraph

poem

story

Complete these sentences:

Name _____

At the end of a

_____, you put a

period. A _____

has a main idea. A

_____ does not have to

rhyme. A _____ has a

beginning, middle, and end.

Practice by tracing the words.
Then write the words.

Name _____

fiction

nonfiction

biography

autobiography

Complete these sentences:

Name _____

A _____ book tells

about things that really

happened. A _____

book tells a story that

is not real.

A _____ tells the

story of someone's life.

Practice Page

Practice writing on your own.

Name _____

Practice Page

Practice writing on your own.

Name _____

Practice writing on your own.

Name _____

Practice writing on your own.

Name _____

Practice writing on your own.

Name _____

Practice writing on your own.

Name _____

Practice by tracing the words.
Then write the words.

Name _____

add

subtract

multiply

divide

Practice by tracing the words.
Then write the words.

Name _____

sum

product

regrouping

Complete this sentence:

When you add, the

answer is called

a _____.

Practice by tracing the words.
Then write the words.

Name _____

one-half

one-fourth

one-eighth

three-quarters

Complete the sentence that best describes the picture.

Name _____

There is _____ glass of milk left. The pizza is _____ gone. There is only _____ of the pizza left.

Practice by tracing the words.
Then write the words.

Name _____

yard

inch

foot

mile

meter

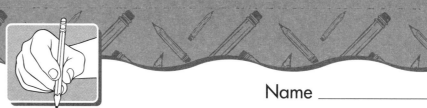

Complete these sentences:

Name _____

There are three feet in

a _____. There are

twelve _____ in a _____.

There are thirty-six

inches in a _____.

There are 1760 yards in

a _____.

Practice by tracing the words.
Then write the words.

Name _____

habitat

experiment

food chain

water cycle

Practice by tracing the words.
Then write the words.

Name _____

paint

draw

sketch

sculpture

Music Words

Practice by tracing the words.
Then write the words.

Name _____

sing

piano

note

strings

Music Words

Practice by tracing the words.
Then write the words.

Name _____

band

violin

drums

trumpet

Practice writing on your own.

Name _____

Practice Page

Practice writing on your own.

Name _____

Practice writing on your own.

Name _____

Practice writing on your own.

Name _____

Thank-You Note

Practice writing a thank-you note.

Name _____

Friendly Letter

Practice writing a letter to your friend.

Name _____

Practice writing on your own.

Name _____

Practice writing on your own.

Name _____